First published by Eulogy For Life 2019

Eulogy For Life
14 Isaacs Street
Busselton, Western Australia 6280
www.eulogyforlife.com

Written by Denise Gibb
Graphic design by Julie Rick
Cover illustration by Austeja Slavickaite
Cartoon illustrations by Denise Gibb

ISBN 978-0-6485446-4-7 (print)
ISBN 978-0-6485446-8-5 (eBook)

Cataloguing-in-Publication data is available from the National Library of Australia.

The Sympathy Gift Series

Healing from Grief
Last Woof
Last Purr
Goodbye Grandma
Goodbye Grandpa

The Sympathy Gift Series offers words of comfort to the bereaved.

Write, email or leave a review online. I'd love to hear how this book comforted you and your family.

sympathygiftseries.com - eulogyforlife.com - denisegibb.com.au

Goodbye Grandma is a beautiful true to life storybook that helps break the news of Grandma's death to children.

Comforting photographs allow gentle and honest conversations about what happens next.

Delightful illustrations encourage younger children to ask questions and express their thoughts and feelings.

Together, the photos, illustrations and words balance the sadness of death with healing strategies the entire family can follow.

For most children, the best way through grief is by doing, talking, and sharing.

Read one-on-one or as a family.

Goodbye Grandma helps parents and children process sadness until happiness returns. (Suits ages 4+)

May Grandma rest in peace.

Paste your favorite photo of your
Grandma here.

(Be sure to choose a photo
that makes you smile.)

Goodbye Grandma

We have some sad news to share. Grandma died.
That means we'll no longer see her beautiful smile
or hear her warm laughter.

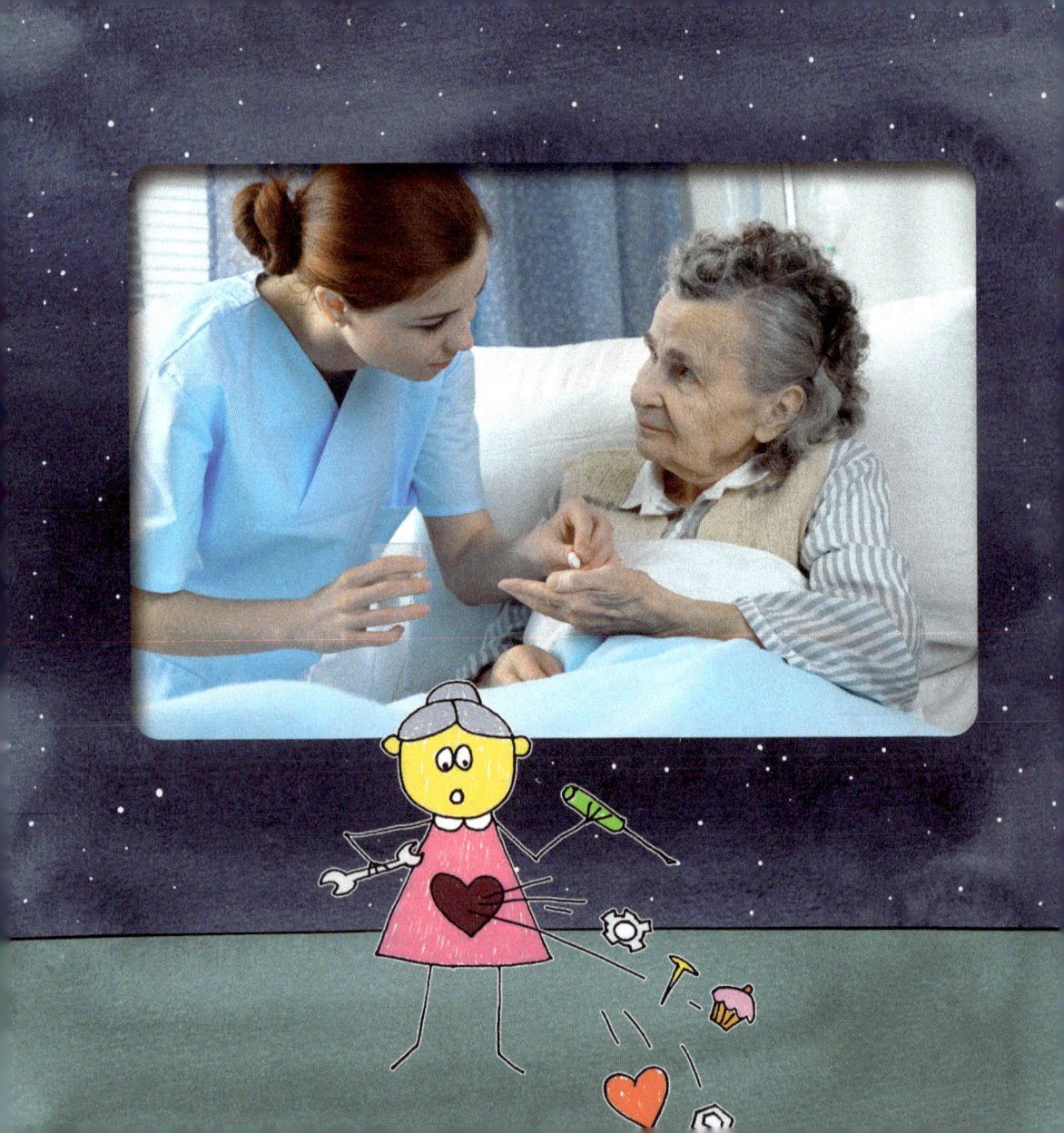

Grandma died because her body stopped working.
A body can stop working because it's old,
extremely sick or broken beyond repair.

Grandma's body is now inside a coffin ready for her funeral.

At the funeral, all those who knew and loved Grandma will gather to say goodbye.

Some people will cry — even mummy and daddy. Others will look sad. But inside we all have happy memories of Grandma.

Your memories of Grandma differ from mine.
But by sharing our stories, we can help each
other remember happy days.

RIP
GRANDMA

Many funerals for Grandmas take place at a cemetery. The coffin is lowered into a hole in the ground called a grave.

Afterwards, families visit their Grandma's grave and leave flowers. But not all funerals are held in a cemetery.

Some families cremate their Grandma and bring home the ashes in a funeral urn.

Many people believe Grandmas go to a special place after they die. Several religions call this place Heaven.

Around the world, Gan Eden, Paradise, Moksha, or Nirvana are other names given to Heaven. No one word is right or wrong.

Our hearts will ache without Grandma in our lives. Some days we'll feel sad, angry, or confused. That's okay.

On sad, angry, or confused days, we need to find
the love Grandma left in our hearts.

We can still talk to Grandma. She'll hear our words, thoughts, and prayers but she won't answer like before.

Sometimes Grandma will visit in our dreams.

Other times we'll hear Grandma's voice
in our minds.

Even though we can't see Grandma anymore,
she'll still watch over us.

In time, the sadness we feel because Grandma died will fade. So, until then...

Let's kiss away each other's tears.

Let's tell each other happy stories about Grandma.

Let's ask the toys if they have questions about Grandma's death.

Let's remember we're still a family even without Grandma.

Let's cry when we need to.

Let's ask for cuddles when we feel sad,
mad, worried or frightened.

Let's surprise each other with big hugs and tickles.

Let's bake Grandma's favourite cake and invite friends over to eat it with us.

Let's play outside and let laughter chase away our sadness.

Let's not be afraid to do new things without Grandma.

Let's keep something of Grandma's in our pocket,
so her love stays close.

Let's show Grandpa new ways to do things now
that he doesn't have Grandma.

Let's draw a big love heart on this page and fill it with kisses to send to Grandma.

Let's grow veggies in a tub and call it Grandma's Garden.

Let's look at the night sky and name a shooting star after Grandma.

Let's close our eyes each night and tell Grandma
our news.

Let's record a video saying what we miss most about Grandma.

Let's make a memorial quilt from Grandma's clothes so we can still feel her hugs.

Let's plan a picnic and take a picture of
Grandma with us.

Let's find shapes in the clouds that remind us of
the love Grandma left in our hearts.

Let's sing our favourite song so loud,
Grandma can hear us in Heaven.

Let's walk in the sunshine in memory of Grandma.

Let's whisper 'Goodnight, Grandma' before we close our eyes to sleep.

Let's remember Grandma wants
us to find happiness again.

Goodbye Grandma.
We'll love you - forever.

Be gently honest when breaking the news of Grandma's death. Child psychologists recommend:

- Use the words dying, dead and died.
- Avoid euphemisms like 'The angels took Grandma' or 'Grandma went to sleep and never woke up'. Young children may fear the angels will come and take other adults they love. Or children may worry about their parents going to sleep and never waking up.
- Be honest and give age-appropriate explanations about why Grandma died.
- Allow children to ask questions and talk about their feelings.
- Display your emotions and talk about how you're processing your grief. (Children will learn from you.)
- Answer all questions about the funeral, burial or cremation.
- Introduce beliefs appropriate to your culture and religion.
- Reassure children death is a natural end to the life cycle.
- Try to include your children in any decision-making that affects them (e.g. adults assigned to care for them if you're too emotionally distraught).
- Inform the school of the death.
- Reassure children it's okay to play and laugh even if the adults are sad.
- Encourage children to express their feelings and ask questions.
- Continue familiar routines (school, sport, walking pets, and household activities).

Adults who model healthy grief behaviour equip children with the skills, strength, and courage to deal with loss. Make Grandma's death a lasting gift of love and learning.

10 Tips for Parents Processing Grief

Processing your loss while modelling healthy grief behaviour to children is challenging. Here are 10 tips to help.

1. Give yourself (and your family) permission to grieve.
2. Take care of yourself (eat a healthy diet and exercise).
3. Give yourself and your family time to adjust (postpone major decisions).
4. Say goodbye and accept your loss.
5. Allow others to help (or ask for help).
6. Surround yourself with positive people.
7. Prepare for events likely to make you sad.
8. Trust you'll pass through grief.
9. Do new things with your family.
10. Remind yourself happy memories are healing memories.

In time, the memory of Grandma will fill everyone's heart with warmth and joy, not sadness*. Until then, talk to your children, extended family, and friends often. Love surrounds you on earth and from Above.

Condolences for your loss.

(*If you feel you are not coping and grief is hampering how you live, or it's affecting your family or work, please seek professional medical help. Severe long-term grief can put your physical, mental and emotional health at risk.)

About the Author

Denise Gibb is an Australian author whose professional writing draws from a rich tapestry of experience.

She's written with Australia's most trusted psychic medium, Mitchell Coombes, to create bestselling titles like *Sensing Spirit* and *Signs from Spirit*.

When working for ABC Radio Denise wrote *Talking in the Streets*—a ten-part drama awarded a gold medal at the New York Festivals.

From print, radio and television through to social media, Denise has written books, resources, advertisements, digital content and more.

Similarly, Denise's unique personal insight into life after death, balancing success with failure and life with loss led to her creating *The Sympathy Gift Series*.

"My desire is to help people use the energy of happy to heal sad."

Denise currently lives in Australia with her partner.

Write, email or leave a review online. Denise would love to hear how this book comforted you and your family.

Find out more at sympathygiftseries.com - eulogyforlife.com - denisegibb.com.au